YOUR KNOWLEDGE HAS VALUE

- We will publish your bachelor's and master's thesis, essays and papers

- Your own eBook and book -
  sold worldwide in all relevant shops

- Earn money with each sale

Upload your text at www.GRIN.com
and publish for free

GRIN

Lisa Jo Elliott

The Role of Analogical Reasoning in Cue Evaluation for First Responders

GRIN Verlag

Bibliografische Information der Deutschen Nationalbibliothek:

Die Deutsche Bibliothek verzeichnet diese Publikation in der Deutschen National-
bibliografie; detaillierte bibliografische Daten sind im Internet über http://dnb.d-
nb.de/ abrufbar.

Imprint:

Copyright © 2014 GRIN Verlag GmbH
Druck und Bindung: Books on Demand GmbH, Norderstedt Germany
ISBN: 978-3-656-71926-7

This book at GRIN:

http://www.grin.com/en/e-book/278252/the-role-of-analogical-reasoning-in-cue-
evaluation-for-first-responders

The Role of Analogical Reasoning in Cue Evaluation for First Responders.

Lisa Jo Elliott

New Mexico State University

Author Note

Lisa Jo Elliott, Department of Psychology, New Mexico State University

Lisa Jo Elliott is now at Missouri Western State University, Department of Psychology.

Acknowledgements. Many thanks to the firefighters and law enforcement officers who gave their time and trust for this study.

This manuscript is based on a doctoral dissertation.

Correspondence concerning this article should be addressed to: Lisa Jo Elliott, Ph.D. Department of Psychology, Missouri Western State University, St. Joseph, MO 64507.

Abstract

During a casual conversation, a law enforcement officer claimed that the type of cues that a novice officer selected determined his/her eventual success in becoming a skilled decision maker. Previous literature in cognition and developmental psychology has suggested a similar phenomenon. Analogical reasoning is correlated to cue evaluation in problem solving and in decision making (Gentner, Holyoak & Kokinov, 2001).

In order to explore this further, a two part study was employed. In the first part, law enforcement officers and firefighters with more than ten years of experience were interviewed about training, cues and standard operating procedures. Then, these officers assisted in creating the testing materials. In the second part, law enforcement and firefighting officers took the test which consisted of an analogy test and an evaluation of important cues within scenarios.

The results of the study suggest that law enforcement officers use analogical reasoning to determine cues within a scenario but firefighters do not. The law enforcement officers who were good at identifying important cues were also good at matching less obvious word meanings. Firefighters who were good at identifying important cues were poor at matching less obvious word meanings.

When the decision making procedures from both sets of subject matter experts were reviewed, firefighters stated that a standard operating procedure based on heuristics is used. Law enforcement officers stated that reasoning skill is a strong component of standard operating procedure. The study produced training recommendations for firefighters and law enforcement officers.

Keywords: Analogical reasoning, Training, Heuristics, Naturalistic Decision Making, Recognition Primed Decision Making, Firefighters, Law Enforcement, First Responder training

The Role of Analogical Reasoning in Cue Evaluation for First Responders.
This study began with a training officer who claimed that the future success of a new officer
can be predicted by observing a new trainee's evaluation of important cues when she/he is
first on the scene. When asked what made a cue important or not, the officer clarified that the
cues were not what he wanted to know more about. The officer wanted to know what sort of
reasoning skill was correlated to the ability to determine important cues and cue judgments
(personal conversation, December 9, 2009). The officer wanted to ensure that the training he
provided to his novice officers included the skill he had observed in successful new officers.

The cognitive psychology literature has touted analogical reasoning as a key
component in cue evaluation as it pertains to problem solving and decision making. However,
few studies have investigated a correlation between analogical reasoning skill and decision
making. Until Gary Klein's work with firefighters in 1989, little was known about how
decision makers operated in their natural environment (Klein, 1989). Klein and colleagues
built a literature of decision making in a natural environment which is termed, *naturalistic
decision making*. Within the literature a standard interviewing technique is used. This
technique is based on the work of Flanagan (1954). It identifies critical stories in which a
decision maker had several decision points from which to choose. These decision points
determine the outcome of the critical story. Klein and colleagues have determined that expert
performance rests on a person's judgment at these crucial points (Klein, Calderwood,
Clinton-Cirocco, 1985). The decision points may be identifiable cues or a confluence of
events or a 'feeling' that a decision maker determines during the situation.

Thus, this study combined Klein's interview methodology with a paper assessment of
skill. This new methodology addresses concerns over validity in field work by triangulation.
The interviews with the subject matter experts were supported by the results of the
participants' paper assessments and the assessments supported the unique standard operating
procedures stated by the experts.

The paper assessments included a standard scenario/cue identification test which is
similar to the promotion tests for both law enforcement and firefighting officers. The
assessment also included an analogical reasoning test. For those readers who are not familiar
with the construct of analogical reasoning, a brief summary of the literature is below.

Analogical Reasoning

Analogical reasoning and problem solving has been well-established as part of the psychology literature for over 30 years. Researchers in analogical reasoning report that analogical problem solving is much like decision making (Gentner, Holyoak & Kokinov, 2001). Analogical reasoning is the mechanism by which experts evaluate and determine the structure of a problem (Dunbar, 2001; Holyoak & Morrison, 2005) and is thought to be the seat of cognition (Hofstadter, 2001). It is likely that analogical reasoning is a mechanism of decision making (Kokinov, 2003). Decision makers are presented with cues, some are important to the solution and some are not important. Evaluation of the important cues frames the decision, determines the schema and guides the strategy evaluation according to Klein, Phillips, Rall and Peluso, (2007).

In analogical problem solving, categorization of a problem's characteristics creates relational shifts in a person's understanding of the cues and their remembrance of the cue associations (Gick & Holyoak, 1980, 1983; Gentner 1983, 1988, 1989; Holyoak & Thagard, 1997; Holyoak & Morrison 2005; Kokinov, 2003). Persons who categorize the cues according to the structure of a problem are better able to transfer a solution from one problem to a similarly structured problem (Catrambone & Holyoak, 1989; Gentner, 1983).

In law enforcement training, the development of reasoning skill receives little attention (personal conversation, December 9, 2009). Often, training focuses primarily on strategies and procedures over a number of cases (personal conversation, December 9, 2009). Learners are expected to pick up the cues which indicate that a procedure that should be applied. As the training officer related, many learners do this task as part of the training, but many learners do not (personal conversation, December 2009). The quality of the officer's decision is determined by her/his proficiency in categorizing cues as important or not important (personal conversation, December 2009).

Several models of decision making stress the importance of meaningful cues during the decision process but fail to specify the mechanism by which this occurs. This mechanism may be analogical reasoning or it may be another mechanism. In the recognition primed decision making model (RPD), Klein discusses how the decision maker must notice meaningful cues and cue patterns from the environment (1989). Klein suggests that an accumulation of remembered situations (i.e., a mass of cues extracted from many individual situations) are stored as frames/schemata. These frames (e.g., yellow smoke, concrete block building, burning hot) feed the decision maker's ability to determine possible outcomes and expectations based on similar past events (e.g., the house cannot be saved, but saving the residential block is possible).

Gentner, Holyoak and Kokinov suggest that a person's ability to derive the important cues is correlated to their ability to derive a satisfactory solution (2001). Catrambone and Holyoak, (1989) and Gentner, (1983) found that if the important cues specific to the problem are noted (e. g. the troops are approaching from one direction only), a person is more likely to notice the structure of the problem. If the person focuses on unimportant cues (e.g. the color of the gun), the wrong cues lead to problem solving error.

Interviews

The officer initiating the research question suggested that the study be restricted to first responders. Preliminary interviews with Emergency Medical Technicians (EMT), Firefighters and Law Enforcement officers determined that Firefighters and Law Enforcement officers would have the most opportunity to make individual decisions during a critical situation. Emergency Medical Technicians within the immediate area were subject to constraints and reported directly to an Emergency Physician at the local hospital for decision making. In addition, the majority of the firefighters were also EMTs. The firefighters requested that either their EMT knowledge or their firefighting knowledge be tested, but not both. In the firefighters' opinions, the firefighting domain offered more individual decision skill opportunity.

The SMEs were interviewed according to the methods suggested in Crandall, Klein, and Hoffman (2006). A single interviewer used a semi-structured interview with the guiding questions listed in Appendix A. In subsequent interviews, the SMEs advised on improvements on the experimental materials, identified the important cues in the scenarios and clarified their previous answers to the interview questions.

Prior to interviewing the subject matter experts or testing the officers, I expected that the officers in both domains would categorize cues as important or not in similar ways. In addition, I expected to find a positive correlation between analogical reasoning skill and the ability to select the important cues in both firefighting and law enforcement. I also expected that the responses to the interview questions would be consistent with the work of Klein and his colleagues (Klein, Calderwood, Clinton-Cirocco, 1985).

Preliminary scenarios were constructed from training materials in law enforcement and firefighting available publicly prior to any discussion with the SMEs (Rubin, 2001; Santangelo, Bovsun, & Zullo, 2002; Montagna, 1999; Schroeder & Lombardo, 2009). These experimental materials were used as a starting point for the discussions with the SMEs. Several SMEs (FF-1, FF-2, LEO-1, LEO-2, LEO-3) remarked that the experimental materials were very similar to performance reviews and advancement tests within their departments. These SMEs believed that the officers would have no trouble completing the materials but that the officers would be suspicious of the underlying motive and may not answer all of the questions.

Methods

Bootstrapping

Bootstrapping is a method of gaining knowledge about a domain so that the researcher understands basic concepts and terminology. Several introductory texts were available through a local institution's firefighting program (Rubin, 2001; Santangelo, Bovsun, & Zullo, 2002; Montagna, 1999). Law enforcement materials were used (Schroeder & Lombardo, 2009).

During the bootstrapping process, I learned that some individuals were paid (career officers) and other individuals volunteered their time because they enjoyed it (volunteer officers). However, volunteers worked only in firefighting. All of the officers in law enforcement were paid.

Participants

The study received approval from the institutional review board with a waiver of written consent. A consent information sheet was used in place of a signed consent form. Gender information was not recorded in order to protect anonymity. Participants were not compensated for the study in any way.

There were three types of participants in the study. These were seven senior training officers- subject matter experts (SMEs), officers (33 firefighters-FF, 13 law enforcement-LEO), and 52 non-FF or non-LEO study participants who were in the same age range as the officers- (controls). The officers and SMEs had been in their profession from three months to over 40 years and ranged in age from 18 years old to over 61 years of age. In law enforcement, the age range started at 24 years old. In firefighting, four different departments participated and those departments were in different areas of the same state in the United States. In law enforcement, two different departments participated from two different states in the United States. Below is a description of the SMEs.

SME FF-1. a Fire Chief who had been a fire ground commander for 15 years and who had 25 years of experience in firefighting.

SME FF- 2. Two captains with over 10 years of experience fighting fires and five years of training experience.

SME FF-3. a volunteer firefighter who had worked at two volunteer Fire Departments for more than 10 years.

Law enforcement. SME LEO-1. Sergeant with over 20 years of experience in law enforcement and 10 years as a training officer.

SME LEO- 2. Lieutenant with over 10 years of experience.

SME LEO- 3. Captain with over 10 years of experience.

Materials

Test materials. The testing materials consisted of demographic questions, the four word analogy test from Elliott (2006), 10 scenarios, and the cues (please see Appendix B and C). In order to ensure validity, more than one SME in each domain reviewed the materials.

For the analogy test, the questions from Elliott, (2006) were used. There are many analogical reasoning studies which use or discuss the validity of the four word analogical matching paradigm to measure analogical reasoning in a psychology lab setting (Green, Fugelsang, Kraemer, Shamosh & Dunbar, 2006; Bassok, Chase & Martin, 1998; Holyoak & Thagard, 1997; Sternberg, 1977; Wisniewski & Bassok, 1999). A portion of the test is in Appendix B. In the firefighter's materials, there were 10 scenarios with 12 - 32 cues to select in each. In the law enforcement materials, there were 10 scenarios with 18 - 26 cues in each scenario.

Procedure

Interview. The SMEs were interviewed for approximately 14 hours in total. The sessions consisted of two- 1 hour meetings discussing the study and asking the guiding questions. Then, there were three- 2 hour sessions with the SMEs to create the scenarios and cues and clarify their previous answers. The SME-LEOs were interviewed for the same number of hours (14 hours in total) in a similar manner. The interview questions are in Appendix A with the answers by topic in Appendix D.

Testing. The SMEs refused to allow their officers to participate without substantial control over the privacy and anonymity of the participating officers. The SMEs requested that no data identifying the officers in any way be collected. The SMEs also requested that the study was administered as either as a voluntary portion of a regular meeting or a voluntary activity that the officer would engage in off-duty.

     Test administration. Officers read an informational consent letter that outlined the risks, benefits and voluntary nature of the study. Their names, locations or any other identifiable information was not collected or included in this study. The study booklets were pre-labeled by random alphanumeric code.

     The SME distributed the paper booklets along with envelopes. The study took approximately one hour. When the officer was finished with the booklet, she or he placed it in the envelope and sealed the envelope. Then, the officer returned the sealed envelope to the SME. After all the testing was complete the SME returned all of the sealed booklets to me in a larger sealed envelope.

     Two departments refused to use this paper version of the study; an identical electronic version of the study was created and administered through a Survey Monkey account (www.surveymonkey.com). Both versions contained the same materials. Subsequent analysis revealed that there was no difference between the answers in the online or paper versions.

     The study materials were given to control participants either in a laboratory on campus or through the online survey. The participants used the same study materials as the officers.

Results

     Many of the officers, in both firefighters and law enforcement, believed that the study had an underlying motive. Many officers filled out only the demographics. It was not possible to replace participants who did not complete the experimental materials. This was expected in the law enforcement officers as law enforcement officers are trained to be suspicious of motive, but it was unexpected in the firefighters (Uttaro, 2002).

     In assessing the results of the analogy testing, the percentage of correct answers was calculated (Elliott, 2006). For the cue evaluations, officers chose either important or not important. This dichotomous categorization approach was used to address the initial training officer's question as it was stated.

     Calculating a percentage correct precludes the ability to detect answering bias or a predetermined answering pattern of important, important, not important, important, important, not important, etc. Thus, the cue evaluation task was assessed using signal detection theory (Green & Swets, 1966; Stanislaw & Todorov,1999). Signal detection theory offers additional analyses to examine bias.

For the cue evaluation, each response was assigned to one of 4 categories:

Hit = If the officer and the SME both categorized the cue as important.

Correct Rejection = If the officer and the SME both categorized the cue as unimportant.

Miss = If the officer categorized the cue as unimportant and the SME categorized the cue as important.

False Alarm = If the officer categorized the cue as important and the SME categorized the cue as unimportant.

Then, the d' and c was calculated according to Stanislaw and Todorov, (1999) and Green and Swets (1966). Finally, d' was used as the predictor variable in a linear regression to model the relationship of cue evaluation to years of service, analogical reasoning, awards and education. First, the results of the linear regression, then the analyses of c will be presented.

Firefighters. The model, $Y = b_0 + X_1 b_1 + X_2 b_2 + X_3 b_3 + X_4 b_4 + X_5 b_5 + e[i]$ with $Y = d'$ of cues was significant; $[F (5, 15) = 3.139, p = 0.039]$. The complete table with beta values are listed in Table 1, the descriptive statistics are in Table 2. The model explained 51% of the variance $[R^2 = 0.511, SE = 0.187]$.

Analogy test was significant with a large effect size $[t = -3.121, p = .007, \eta^2 = 0.88]$. However, analogy test was negatively correlated to the d' score $[r (21) = -0.44, p = .023]$. The unexpected result makes sense in terms of the SME's interview answers in the next section.

Table 1. Regression Model examining the correlates for Firefighters, full model.

Model	Unstandardized Coefficients		Standardized Coefficients	t values	Significance
	B	$SE\ B$	B		
Constant	1.703	0.232		7.346	0.000
Analogy*	-1.035	0.449	-0.683	-2.304	0.035
Years of Experience	-0.001	0.004	-0.054	0.236	0.816
Education	0.025	0.034	0.206	0.739	0.471
Awards	-0.172	0.128	-0.325	-1.345	0.197

Note: * $p < .05$, ** $p < .01$.

Table 2. Descriptive Statistics for Firefighters

	Mean	St. Dev.	Range	Correlation to d'
Age	27	11	18 – 61	-0.302**
Years of Service	9.45	12.31	0.08 – 40	- 0.197
Years of College	3.85	1.88	0 – 8	-0.208
Analogy Score	0.61	0.213	0.35 to 0.89	- 0.44*

$n = 21$ * $p < .05$, ** $p < .10$.

Law enforcement officers. The model, $Y = b_0 + X_1\ b_1 + X_2\ b_2 + X_3\ b_3 + X_4\ b_4 + X_5\ b_5 + e[i]$ with $Y = d'$ of cues was significant $[F\ (1, 11) = 9.84, p = .009]$. The complete table with beta values is listed in Table 3; the descriptive statistics are listed in Table 4. The model explained 78% of the variance $[R^2 = 0.779, SE = 0.139]$.

Analogy test was significant with a large effect size $[t = 3.08, p = .02, \eta^2 = .86]$. A significant positive correlation was found between the d' score and the analogy score $[r\ (13) = 0\ .687, p = .005]$. Officers who did well in the analogy task also did well in the cue evaluation task.

Table 3 Regression Model examining the correlates for Law Enforcement Officers, full model

	Unstandardized Coefficients		Standardized Coefficients	t values	Significance
Model	B	$SE\ B$	β		
Constant	-1.89	.80		-2.36	.05
Analogy*	2.58	.84	1.148	3.08	.018
Age*	-.04	.01	-1.354	-2.68	.032
Years of Experience	-0.03	.03	-.322	-1.3	.235
Education	.11	.14	.229	.77	.467
Awards*	.03	.01	1.513	2.66	.032

Table 4. Descriptive Statistics for Law Enforcement Officers

	Mean	St. Dev.	Range	Correlation to d'
Age	34	10	24 – 61	-0.394
Years of Service	10.5	8.68	4-25	-0.197*
Years of College	4.3	1.84	0 – 8	0.143
Analogy Score	.60	0.17	0.43 – 0.82	0.687*

$n = 13$ * $p < .05$, ** $p < .10$.

Controls. The control participants who took the same test, performed significantly differently from the officers [t (61) = 6.717, $p < .0001$, Cohen's d = -0.43]. In the controls, no relationship was found between analogy score and the cue importance rating [r = -0.16, p = ,633]. A Pearson correlation between age in non-experts and analogy score did not find a significant relationship between the years a person has lived and their analogical reasoning ability [r = 0.243, p = .099].

Response bias. In order to calculate if a response bias, a sensitivity measure of c was calculated for each officer. According to Beauchamp (2010), large (> 1.0) values of c signal a response bias. As the value of c approaches zero, a response bias is not present.

The officers did not have a value of c which exceeded 1.0. For the firefighters, mean = 0.217, standard deviation = 0.72, standard error = 0.17; for the law enforcement officers section, mean = -0.57, standard deviation = 0.21, standard error = 0.05. There was no response bias.

Summary. The central analysis of the correlation between cue evaluation and analogical reasoning found that firefighters had a negative correlation and law enforcement officers had a positive correlation. Both correlations were significant. Firefighters had a mean d' score of 1.386 ($SD = 0.92$, $SE = 0.22$); the law enforcement officers had a mean d' score of 0.45 ($SD = 0.23$, $SE = 0.056$). None of the law enforcement officers obtained a perfect d' score. Three of the firefighters obtained perfect d' scores.

The three firefighters accurately evaluated all of the cues. These officers were from departments different from the SMEs and had not seen the material previous to testing. Yet, none of the law enforcement officers accurately evaluated all of the cues but it was significantly positively correlated to reasoning. Clearly this indicates that there are strong differences in cue evaluation between the domains.

Discussion

It is possible that the law enforcement training officer was correct in the assertions that the future success of a new recruit could be assessed by observing her/his ability to evaluate cues as important or not. But the SME interviews reveal additional information which clarifies how cues are selected and the role of standard operation procedures.

Interview results. In the interviews with the SMEs, the SME-FF stated that the firefighters follow a distinct method of analyzing each situation for cues. In general, the SME-FF described that firefighters apply a standard operating procedure of descending importance when they are first to arrive at an incident. This guides their evaluation of important cues. The standard operating procedure for firefighting was reported to be- 1.) Location, 2.) Type of Incident, and 3.) Quality of Fire. These responses are in Appendix D. If the SME-FF applied a standard operating procedure to all of the cues in each scenario, a perfect d' score would be easy to achieve. A high analogical reasoning score would not be needed if the standard operating procedures were used.

Cue Evaluation

Firefighting. In firefighting, the SME-FFs stated that the first team on the scene has the primary objective of maintaining control and keeping the situation stable. First on the scene firefighters use the standard operating procedure to determine the most important things to attend to and then delay other decisions until a more senior officer arrives to take command. Once a more senior officer arrives to take command, she/he must immediately understand what decisions have been made and why. A set of standard operating procedures fulfills this requirement.

The SME-FF stated that the standard operating procedures (SOP) were put into place to discourage individual decision making during a fire event. In addition to official procedures which dictate the use of the SOP, social pressure within the department discourages deviation from the SOP. Officers who deviate from the standard operating procedure during training or a fire event (and 'think for themselves') are disciplined and labeled as, "rogue firefighters" (see Appendix D). In addition, the SME-FF stated that firefighters who did not follow the SOP and seemed to "read too much into it" were encouraged to try another profession. "We don't need any heroes, we need firefighters who will work together like a well-oiled machine; we need a team." In a conversation with a fire ground commander who has 35 years of service, "We work off of an S. O. P. [standard operating guidelines] that it [sic] set by the board and the fire chief [,] if some[thing] go[goes] wrong[,] it has to go to the chief and he take[s] [it] to the fire board for it to be adopted" (personal email, March 4, 2011).

The research literature also supports these perspectives. Lipshitz, Omodei, McClellan, and Wearing (2007), discuss the frequency of standard operating procedures in firefighters' decision making:

> "The standard operating procedures established in Firefighting organizations… are highly specific and routinized. … Specific jobs or roles within the system are specialized and guided by standard operating procedures… Consequently, firefighters' uncertainty falls into two decision categories: (a) deciding which procedure applies to the given case, but then deciding how to adjust the standard procedure to the situation at hand, and (b) deciding how to cope with uncertainty that is not covered by available procedures" (p. 100).

Therefore, the factors of education, commendations, years of service and analogical reasoning do not directly affect cue evaluation. Instead, all of these factors are filtered through the SOPs. The standard operating procedures guide the selection of cues.

Figure 1. The role of SOP in FF cue evaluation.

In a model of how the SOP would work in Firefighting, let X_{ar} = analogical reasoning, X_{com}= commendations or awards, X_{yrs} = years of service, X_{ed}= years of education, the dotted circle of SOP = standard operating procedure, Y d' = selecting the correct cues to guide the decision for the next course of action.

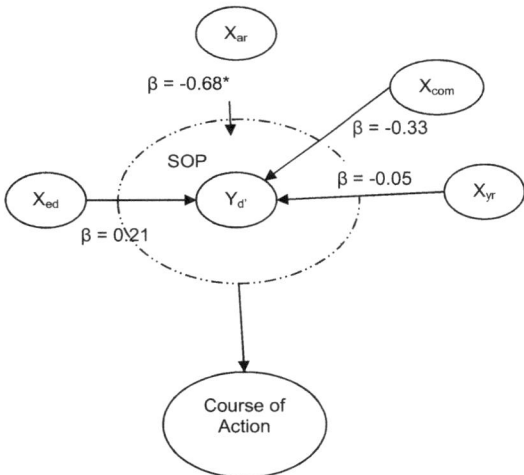

Law enforcement. Unlike firefighting, the law enforcement officer who is first on the scene holds primary decision making authority until the situation is resolved. He or she is responsible for conveying the important cues to other officers as they assist in the investigation. The officer who was first on the scene maintains the primary decision making role regardless of rank because this officer witnessed the cues when the scene was the 'freshest' (personal conversation, December 9, 2009). If an officer was to evaluate each situation using reasoning and without applying a standard operating procedure, a perfect *d'* score would be difficult to achieve but a high analogical reasoning score would be easy to achieve.

The standard operating procedures are implemented *after* the cue evaluation (see Appendix D). Law enforcement officers who are just arriving on a call are encouraged to "follow your gut" and use his/her intuition. As a SME-LEO stated, "In law enforcement, there are not types of people, you cannot predict who will commit a crime. Law enforcement officers know that given the right circumstances any individual is able to commit any crime".

This is consistent with what Feltovich, Spiro, and Coulson (1989) suggest. Law enforcement officers deal with boundless contingencies. As LEO-2 and LEO-1 stated, "There is no such thing as a typical call" "The human element, there are millions of possibilities". The boundless contingencies require that law enforcement officers use analogical reasoning to determine cues instead of a standard operating procedure. The number of standard operating procedures needed to account for every contingency would be infinite.

Therefore, analogical reasoning impacts cue evaluation in law enforcement. The heuristics within SOPs guide the decision maker as to the next course of action *after* the cue evaluation. The cues determine which SOP applies and narrows the possible contingencies for the officer.

Figure 2. The role of SOP in LEO cue evaluation.

In a model of how the SOP would work in Law Enforcement, let X_{ar} = Analogical Reasoning, X_{com}= commendations or awards, X_{yrs} = years of service, X_{ed} = years of education, the circle of SOP = standard operating procedure, Y d' = selecting the correct cues to guide the decision for the next course of action.

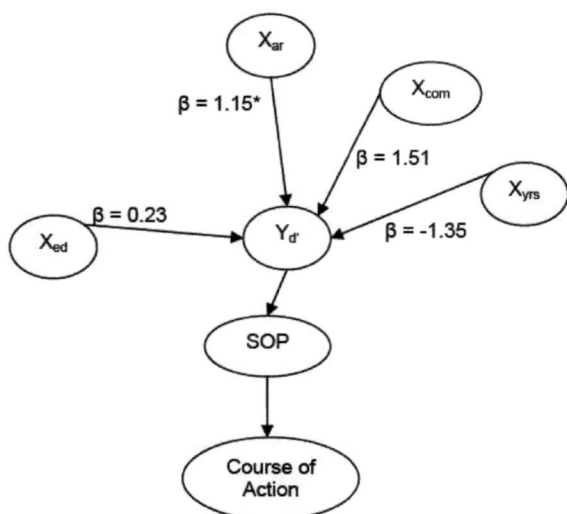

Analogues or Analogical Reasoning

Analogues should not be confused with analogical reasoning. The use of an analogue does not rely on the evaluation of the structure of the problem. Analogues rely on the ability to remember a situation's features and match those features to a situation with similar features. Analogical reasoning relies on the ability to evaluate the problem and its cues in their connection to each other and to the problem structure. The relation of the cues is of primary importance. It is the relations that is remembered and constitutes analogical reasoning (Gentner, 1983).

For example, Captain Sully Sullenberger learned the structure of aviation crashes through years as an accident investigator. Within the structure, he learned the cues to "watch out for" and how they related (Stark & Barrett, 2009). The relations between the cues become well known through hundreds of trials as demonstrated in Juslin, Olsson, and Olsson (2003).

Impact

At the conclusion of the study, the results were shared with the participating departments. As a result, the law enforcement training officer implemented analogical reasoning evaluations and encouraged officer training in reasoning skill. The firefighting departments have implemented increased testing on the standard operating procedures.

The results of this study suggest that written tests of analogical reasoning may be useful for predicting cue evaluation in some domains but should not be universally applied across all domains. In order to determine which domains are appropriate for an analogical reasoning test, an in-depth interview can help determine how and at what stage does the domain implement the SOPs. The questions listed in Appendix A were very successful at encouraging the SMEs to talk candidly about cue evaluation, decisions, judgment, and training. Some SMEs shared more than others. Three to four SMEs worked well. At three SMEs, the same themes within the domain started to repeat (Appendix D).

Analogical reasoning in naturalistic decision making and cue evaluation needs further work in order to identify the domains where a correlation is present and how it relates to the domain. Additional questions of self-selection into a career based on existing analogical reasoning skill, the relationship between years of experience and analogical reasoning, and the relationship between cue change and analogical reasoning warrants further work. It is the hope of this author that this study will inspire a methodology for investigating these and other questions in many other domains.

18

References

Bassok, M., Chase, V.M., Martin, S.A., (1998). Adding apples and oranges: alignment of semantic and formal knowledge. *Cognitive Psychology 35*, 99–134.

Catrambone, R., & Holyoak, K. (1989). Overcoming contextual limitations on problem-solving transfer. *Journal of experimental psychology: Learning, memory, and cognition, 15* (6), 1147-1156.

Crandall, B., Klein, G. & Hoffman, R. (2006). *Working minds: A practitioner's guide to cognitive task analysis.* Cambridge, MA: The MIT Press.

Dunbar, K. (2001). The Analogical Paradox: Why Analogy is so Easy in Naturalistic Settings, yet so Difficult in the Psychological Laboratory. In D. Gentner, K. J. Holyoak & B. Kokinov (Eds.), *Analogy: Perspectives from cognitive science*. MIT Press. Cambridge, MA.

Elliott, L. J. (2006). Induction of analogical problem solving and predictive measures of solution success. (Master's thesis). Retrieved from the New Mexico State University, Las Cruces, New Mexico.

Feltovich, P.J., Spiro, R.J., & Coulson, R.L. (1989). The nature of conceptual understanding in biomedicine: The deep structure of complex ideas and the development of misconceptions. In D.A. Evans & V.L. Patel (Eds.), *The cognitive sciences in medicine: Biomedical modeling.* Cambridge, MA: MIT Press

Flanagan, J. C. (1954). The critical incident technique. *Psychological Bulletin, 51*(4), 327.

Gick, M. L., & Holyoak, K. J. (1980). Analogical problem solving. *Cognitive psychology, 12*(3), 306-355.

Gick, M. L., & Holyoak, K. J. (1983). Schema induction and analogical transfer. *Cognitive psychology, 15*(1), 1-38.

Gentner, D. (1983). Structure-mapping: A theoretical framework for analogy. *Cognitive science, 7*(2), 155–170.

Gentner, D. (1988). Metaphor as structure mapping: The relational shift. *Child development. 59*, 49-59.

Gentner, D. (1989). The mechanisms of analogical learning. *Similarity and analogical reasoning, 199*, 241.

Gentner, D., Holyoak, K. & Kokinov, B. (2001). *The analogical mind: Perspectives from cognitive science.* Cambridge, MA: The MIT Press.

Gentner, D. & Markman, A. B. (1997). Structure mapping in analogy and similarity. *American Psychologist, 52*, 45-56.

Green, A. E., Fugelsang, J. A., Kraemer, D. J., Shamosh, N. A., & Dunbar, K. N. (2006). Frontopolar cortex mediates abstract integration in analogy. *Brain research, 1096*(1), 125-137.

Green, D. M., & Swets, J. A. (1966). *Signal detection theory and psychophysics.* NY, NY: Wiley. Reprinted in 1974 by Krieger, Huntington, NY.

Hofstadter, D. R. (2001). Epilogue. In D. Gentner, K. J. Holyoak, & B. N. Kokinov (Eds.), *The analogical mind: Perspectives from cognitive science.* (pp. 499-539). Cambridge, MA: MIT Press.

Holyoak, K. J. & Morrison, T. (Eds.) (2005). *The Cambridge handbook of thinking and reasoning.* Cambridge, UK: Cambridge University Press.

Holyoak, K.J., & Thagard, P., (1995). *Mental leaps: Analogy in creative thought.* Cambridge, MA: MIT Press/Bradford Books.

Juslin, P., Olsson, H., & Olsson, A. (2003). Exemplar effects in categorization and multiple-cue judgment. *Journal of experimental psychology: General, 132*(1), 133-156.

Klein, G. A. (1989). Recognition-primed decisions. In W. B. Rouse (Ed.), *Advances in man-machine system research*, (p. 47-92). Greenwich, CT: JAI Press, Inc.

Klein, G. A., Calderwood, R. & Clinton-Cirocco, A. (1985). *Rapid decision making on the fire ground.* Fairborn, OH: Klein Associates.

Klein, G., Phillips, J. K., Rall, E. L., & Peluso, D. A. (2007). A data-frame theory of sensemaking. In R. R. Hoffman (Ed.) *Expertise out of context: Proceedings of the sixth international conference on naturalistic decision making* (pp. 113-155). NY,NY: Lawrence Erlbaum Associates.

Kokinov, B. (2003). Analogy in decision-making and social interaction and emergent rationality. *Behavioral and brain sciences, 26*, 167-168.

Lipshitz, R., Omodei, M., McClellan, J., & Wearing, A. (2007). What's burning? The RAWFS heuristic on the fire ground. In R. R. Hoffman (Ed.) *Expertise out of context:*

Proceedings of the sixth international conference on naturalistic decision making (pp. 97-112). NY,NY: Lawrence Erlbaum Associates.

Montagna, F. C. (1999). *Responding to routine emergencies*. Tulsa, OK: PennWell Books.

Rubin, D. (2001). *Rube's rules for survival: A collection of case studies*. Tulsa, OK: Pennwell Books.

Santangelo, M., Bovsun, M., & Zullo, A. (2002). *The greatest firefighter stories never told*. Riverside, NJ: Andrews McMeel Publishing.

Schroeder, D. J., Lombardo, F. A. (2009). *Barron's police officer exam*. (8th ed). Hauppauge, New York: Barron's Educational Series.

Stark, L. & Barrett, K. (2009). Capt. Sully Sullenberger recounts landing on Hudson River. *ABC News Travel*. Retrieved from http://abcnews.go.com/Travel/story?id=7793478&page=1

Stanislaw, H., & Todorov, N. (1999). Calculation of signal detection theory measures. *Behavior Research Methods, Instruments & Computers, 31*(1), 137-149.

Sternberg, R., (1977). *Intelligence, information processing, and analogical reasoning*. Hillsdale, NJ: Lawrence Erlbaum Associates Inc.,.

Uttaro, M. T. (2002). Naturalistic decision making in law enforcement practice- Exploring the process. Unpublished doctoral dissertation, Virginia Polytechnic Institute and State University. Blacksburg, Virginia.

Wisniewski, E.J., & Bassok, M., (1999). What makes a man similar to a tie? Stimulus compatibility with comparison and integration. *Cognitive Psychology, 39*, 208–238.

Appendix A

The guiding questions for the qualitative interview were as follows:

1. How does training happen in your domain (mentoring, formal academies, books, videos, seminars, is training ongoing)?
2. How are trainees assessed for their knowledge of the domain?
3. How long do they train for before initially entering the domain?
4. How are decisions made when you are on the scene?
5. Are any decisions made before you arrive?
6. Are any decision made after the scene/event has resolved?
7. Who makes decisions?
8. How is the decision quality judged?
9. Are there any repercussions for poor outcomes?
10. What happens when someone makes a "bad" decision?
11. What happens when someone makes a "good" decision?
12. What are your thoughts on cue noticing and its relationship to decisions?

Appendix B

Analogy test

For this section, I need a measure of relationships between things. This type of skill might be related to how you were trained, how you naturally think or your expertise. Please select the bst answer to complete the sequence. The first one is done for you as an example.

Seek is to avoid as...

- € Seek is to Find
- € Pretend is to Win
- € Search is to Treasure
- € Embarrass is to Shun

Germ is to Disease as...

- € Trichinosis is to Pork
- € Doctor is to Medicine
- € Biologist is to Cell
- € Men is to Women
- € War is to Destruction

Firefighter Scenario.

City Fire is requested to respond to a mutual aid fire on County Rd 672 for an oil burner fire in the town of Monso. It has escalated to a full-blown fire. The first two engines had each stretched out their 2.5-inch hand line and were trying to get down the basement located in the front of the building. The heat was so intense that they couldn't advance, and they were operating their hose lines into the basement, attempting to cool it down. Hot, black smoke was pouring out of the cellar. As E-302 is awaiting orders, the smoke changes from black to pearly white. Other teams are on the first floor searching for victims and extension. Another firefighter has just entered the second floor from a portable ladder.

1. As the incident commander, what would your first course of action be?
2. What would suggest this course of action?
3. If this were different, what would be the alternative course of action?

Firefighter Cue Rating Example

After each scenario, please categorize the following items as to their importance in your decision for the scenario.

County Road 672   Town of Monso
  I m portant   I m portant
  N ot I mportant   N ot I mportant

Oil burner fire   Mutual aid fire
  I m portant   I m portant
  N ot I mportant   N ot I mportant

Appendix C

Law Enforcement Scenario.

      For this section, I need to know what cues help you make decisions. Please read the scenario, then tell me what you would do next if you were the officer described. Then, turn the page and categorized the items contained in the scenario. Please do not refer back to the scenario after you turn the page. You may or may not be familiar with the locations. There are ten scenarios in total.

  Scenario 1

      It is 8:26 pm when you hear the dispatcher activate the emergency tone, "Shooting, 2502 E. 19th. Two-five-zero-two East 19th. It's a family disturbance situation. Male was shot by his wife. 24 ADAM and 24 BOSTON and 24 SAM, Code 3. Female suspect still has the weapon. The victim is collapsed on the driveway. Suspect should be alone in the house at this time." You are one of the units who is close to the area. Over the radio, Officer McNally says, "Units going 10-23 set perimeter and secure it. Do we have a 21 for the suspect's residence?" Officer Mariscal then says, "Female should be in the house by herself. There may be a dog also. The third house is the third house east of Smith Blvd on the south side. At this point, there is no activity at the front."

      1. What would your first course of action be?

      2. What would suggest this course of action?

      3. If this were different, what would be the alternative course of action?

Law Enforcement Cue Rating Example

After each scenario, please categorize the following items as to their importance in your decision for the scenario.

Shooting   2501 East 19th
  I m portant   I m portant
  N ot I mportant   N ot I mportant

Male victim   Family disturbance
  I m portant   I m portant
  N ot I mportant   N ot I mportant

Wife perpetrator   She is alone
  I m portant   I m portant
  N ot I mportant   N ot I mportant

Dog   South side of the block
  I m portant   I m portant
  N ot I mportant   N ot I mportant

Appendix D

Responses to the interview questions.

	Firefighter	Law Enforcement
Cues during an event	FF-1- Standard but room to make decisions (fire command). FF-2 "don't let the blood suck you in" if you focus on the bleeding, you miss the most important points should have focused on the other parts. Gunshot, focus on the would, if you're not breathing... We are constantly reviewing cases. FF-1 Looking for the seed of the fire. Surround and drown is the way to go. There is a Fire Triangle of fuel, air, and heat. Remove one and the fire goes out	LEO-2- Cues always changing, never typical. We pull up the SOP from the cues. The human element, there are millions of possibilities. The behavior of the person for where this is headed most. Behavior cues tell us if it will be an easy arrest or a hard arrest. So many possible decisions, there is an SOP with each decision. For some, measure decision making and instinct. Some [officers] have large amounts of experience and can't make a decision
Planning	FF-2- We do lots of pre-planning and review after the event to help with the next one. FF-1 You need to know where the fire is, how it acts, the building age (building codes in the 1970's vs. the 2008 are very different). There are no such things as easiest or most difficult to fight fires. FF-2 When the minute bell goes off, we do a risk vs benefit analysis. Where are we going? Incident" evaluating risk to self and the rewards We will risk a lot to save a lot. No one survives the fire, don't go in to retrieve a corpse. Offensive vs defensive based. Offensive (life save and get to the life) or defensive (surround and drown). Size up, draw a mental picture of what is happening. Where is it going, what is it, what are there any things that will cause danger and loss of life? What is this neighborhood like? Who are the onlookers (are any dangerous, is there an arsonist?) We want to do building walk throughs before they catch on fire. But it's getting more dangerous for us. Someone called a building on fire, the Fire Chief shows up and was ambushed and shot. There are meth labs, booby	LEO-1- We cannot do any pre-planning, we try to keep the worst from happening, we cannot review. LEO-2- There are calls that you are trained for and calls that you are unlikely to be trained for. We never read about police work. There is no such thing as a typical call

	trapped houses. FF-2 When we arrive, we use a SOP which goes like this: 1. Life; 2. Involvement of the fire; 3. Our resources, number of people we have; 4. How much is salvageable; 5. Risk factor, we will risk a lot to save a life whether it is save-able or not; 6. How much of the property is salvageable if less than 50% then it's not salvageable. 7. Do we have enough resources? A lot of officers try to be a hero. Are you a hot dog? Or are you realistic and are not going to try to die at this one? There are a lot of things that people think we should do that we know not to, like hosing a roof down when there is a fire in the attic. This is a bad situation and will make the roof collapse. Certain roofs have specific constructions. This is important to know. You can read the color of the smoke and that will give you information about the construction materials and what is actually burning. We prioritize 1. Life and safety, 2. Property, 3. Mitigation of further damage. Experience is more than years of service, it is years getting feedback on the job. Knowing the community, the way the houses were built, and located.	
Prior knowledge	FF-1- Vast knowledge of fire behavior based on previous building inspections done by the fire department personnel and prior fires. Fire has predictable behavior	LEO-1- Little prior knowledge of possibilities as event unfolds. Humans have unpredictable behavior.
Judgment of Event Outcome	FF-1- Clearly right (fire out, lives saved) or wrong (fire burns, deaths). We know by the end of the event if the decisions that were made during the event were right or not. FF-2 Novice errors are in not following the risk assessment guidelines. A novice firefighter took the fire truck (500 gal) out by himself to a propane fire. When he arrived at the fire he did not establishing another water source.	LEO-1- We never know. In law enforcement, decisions are not right/wrong because outcome is unknown. It must go through the legal system, jury, evidence, detective decisions. LEO-3 - Police don't talk about all that happens. When you are new, you run out of options quickly because you don't know, you haven't learned. When you are

He should have hooked it up to a hydrant first. He forgot his training and soon the truck was out of water and the propane fire got the truck too. Sometimes, they get sucked in by the blood and gore and forget. He ignored the first step in the SOP- life. He didn't hook up the hydrant. We are not allowed to go in unless we have a secure water supply and there is a rescue team to rescue us. There must be two people in to rescue a life. He is lucky he didn't lose his life. When we arrive on the scene, there are usually four firemen on the truck. The driver who only drives the truck; the lieutenant who first takes command and sizes up the situation. He has command until a higher ranking officer arrives. #3 firefighter assists with the water supply. #4 firefighter is the right hand of the lieutenant and drags the hose out and is the nozzleman. The first guy knows to jump off and get the hydrant the back guys know their job, they know from training what is expected of them. We do lots of pre-planning. New OSHA rules state that the Firefighters must be in pairs. They must have a certain number of years of experience between them as a team. No one goes in alone or tries a rescue without a team outside. There must be at least 2 outside. They try to have water on before they go in, but sometimes not if they think they can get out. There is no rank in the command system in firefighting, the most qualified person takes command if the only decision that you can make is to keep people away. That is fine. When a more experienced person arrives the command passes. All the decisions come from that person in charge and pass up as more senior people arrive. Incident command, don't get in trouble and set the stage up for a big performance. A bad decision up front makes a problem that cannot be fixed. Back up, take time to make a decision. When a call comes in, prepare

experienced, you have more options.

mentally, what's happening, where are we going, if going to the county, where am I going to get water? Who is going to help if out of district? If a big building, who do I call for help? May not have the resources to put it out, then let it burn. 1. Life- keep everyone away, let everyone know, paint a picture of what is going on. Each department has operating guidelines that consist of standard operating procedures and guidelines, every position has predetermined jobs, guides, everything. These are the procedures to follow step by step. Guidelines- leeway, guidances. If you do the operating procedures, you don't need commanding officers. For all fires, we know the start, we know the end, we must figure out the middle.

Decision making	FF-2- As soon as the call comes over the loudspeaker in the firehouse; we are planning and make decisions. We are deciding where to put the fire truck, what is the construction of that building, are there going to be occupants during this time of day, … What types of equipment we might need right away. Drilled like the soldiers. Few actual decisions, if you do the operating procedures, you don't need command. All firefighters who are first on a scene are trained to 'take command' or implement the SOP. You don't want someone making it worse.	LEO-1- No one calls us and tells us that a crime is about to be committed. We get calls but usually it is too late. The criminals don't wait to be caught. When we get to a scene, we must decide where to be and whom to investigate on 'hunches'. 'Hunches' make a good or bad cop. Bad cops ignore their intuitions. Decision making is crucial, when to seek more information, decide who the perpetrator most likely is, if the behavior is actionable (the arrest of this person most likely lead to charges). LEO-3– if A then B, B is the reason for the action not collective decision like in firefighting, visual stimuli cue the action. B elicits the LEO response. OODA loop- observe, orient, decide, action. LEO-3- Same game, different levels of emotional involvement. Police must be ahead of the curve, read danger cues, not shoot X live, shoot to prevent. After the violent stage, stay alive.

Locale	FF-2- Trained and practice within the same location entire life. Specially trained for weather, building construction, local behavior	LEO-3- Train and practice at same location. Rarely move because familiar with local laws and local citizens. But, can move.
	FF-1. Must have local scenarios for the locale based on common equipment and common structures and local culture. (what local people know).	
Training procedures	FF-3-Academy, internship, full status, periodic performance reviews for promotion into non-firefighting administrative roles. Constant training on equipment, fire behavior, procedure. Review of events immediately after they happen with positive and negative feedback shared with the group.	LEO-1- Academy, internship, full status. Periodic performance reviews and qualifying exams to continue to practice as a law enforcement officer. Periodic training at department and offsite on new weaponry, procedures. Review of events rarely happens unless a negative outcome (civilian shot).
	FF-2 [A person with] three yrs would be a novice, six years would be an apprentice, 10 yrs to a lieutenant or captain. 100 calls per month. We don't rate people by rank because it is no reflection on expertise. Some officers want stagnant positions others want administration and to go up the promotion ladder. The firefighters on the ground with the hose and camera in hat make small decisions on the ground. The commander stays in the truck and watches. A lot of guys want to be on the ground fighting the fire. They don't want to go into administration and sit in the truck. Many firefighters will fail written tests but be very good out in the field.	LEO-3- different municipalities within the municipality. The academy training is very general, might be anywhere. All police officers training requirement through the dept. of public safety. Then all mentor based. We have in-service which is informal training. Sometimes one officer will go to training and come back and give a brief training. Trained until a proficiency test passed or sometimes given an extension (passed within next 5-10 years). Sometimes we do a beginning pre-test and posttest.
	Firefighting is very competitive now. You must have a college degree and experience, you must have math, and we have a lot of returning vets.	
	The driver doesn't fight the fire, he only drives the truck. The national standard is that there are 4 people to one engine. A double engine can have 7-8 people.	
	FF-2 It used to be that firefighters came from families of firefighter, now it seems that everyone wants to be a firefighter. It's very competitive. The	

31

	guys coming back from Iraq are perfectly trained to be firefighters. Equipment military protocol, strength, and good at following orders. FF-2 We have a knowledge bank filled with scientific and technical information about combustible material, building construction, ventilation and sprinkler systems, electrical circuitry, chemical reactions.	
Training goals	FF-2 Trainers assert standard answers (everyone the same) military based command structure FF-1 We use the mentor and experience model. You cannot learn to fight fires through book learning. As a firefighter, you need all of your senses to be there. Many firefighters will be terrible at the written scenarios but good out in the field. FF-1 Firefighters are much more educated about what involved, much more of a science, what will go boom and what will sizzle. Plastics make fires more toxic, explosive.	LEO-2- As soon as you drop your guard, the person could be the Unabomber- you must be on your guard all the time. Pounded in how to respond instincts at what level to respond, "what if" scenarios are pounded in. Firefighters have constant training, police; all of the training is upfront. LEO-1- Training- 20 hrs per year. State mandated. However, we do 40-80 hours per year. LEO-3- says that you are never the expert; move through your professional career; learning academy; passed test; 12 weeks of field training. FIREFIGHTER short incident commander, gotten input from safety officer watch to be sure follow plan. Use of force control model in a linear fashion. LEO is different because of the unlimited permutations. We give them categories instead of SOP. Then give them scenarios to work through to give them off of the linear. To seasoned officers, this is second nature. LEO-3- Demand for LEO, we looked for visualization- not testing for it so have to train it. Officers who have been there will be more successful but doesn't have to be real. Think through to success. LEO-3- Sheepdog= LEO; Wolf=criminal; Sheep= public; Officers like to use it. You know

		your flock, you know what is normal for the local culture and what is not. Officer survival books and another training model, point out that officers who follow the Sheepdog, Wolf, and Sheep model will not put people in those categories because he was 'such a nice guy'. However, we teach our officers that given the right circumstances any person is capable of any action.